AF487926

Nose Your Animals

This fun children's book
was created through
the imagination of three
young minds:
Henley, Hudson, and Hollis

Is BIG

Has tail

Makes milk

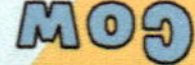

Eat bugs

Is a reptile

Has tongue

Iguana

Likes mud

Snorts

Has curly tail

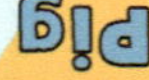

Has whiskers
Swims
Eats small fish
seal

Has wool

Spits

Eats grass

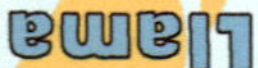

Loves nuts

Climbs trees

Has whiskers

Wags tail

Loves toys

BIG or small

Loves to play

Walks on 4 legs

Has 10 fingers

Baboon

Purrs

Has tail

Says "meow"

Loves apples

Has hooves

Has a mane

Has wool
Lives in herds
Eats plants
sheep

Small

Has long tail

Loves cheese

Mouse

Is tall

Has long neck

Eats leaves

Has a mane

Roars

Has tail

Lion

Very fast

Has pointed ears

Eats plants and small animals

Has talons

Hoots

Can fly

IMO